D1542719

REVENANTS

REVENANTS

poems by

MARK NOWAK

COFFEE HOUSE PRESS :: MINNEAPOLIS 2000

COPYRIGHT © 2000 Mark Nowak
COVER PHOTOGRAPH © Mark Nowak
AUTHOR PHOTOGRAPH © Carloyn Erler
COVER + BOOK DESIGN Linda S. Koutsky

COFFEE HOUSE PRESS is an independent nonprofit literary publisher supported in part by a grant provided by the Minnesota State Arts Board, through an appropriation by the Minnesota State Legislature, and in part by a grant from the National Endowment for the Arts. Significant support has also been provided by the Bush Foundation; Elmer L. & Eleanor J. Andersen Foundation; General Mills Foundation; Honeywell Foundation; James R. Thorpe Foundation; Lila Wallace-Reader's Digest Fund; McKnight Foundation; Medtronic; Pentair, Inc.; Patrick and Aimee Butler Family Foundation; the law firm of Schwegman, Lundberg, Woessner & Kluth, P.A.; The St. Paul Companies Foundation, Inc.; Star Tribune Foundation; the Target Foundation; West Group; and many individual donors. To you and our many readers across the country, we send our thanks for your continuing support.

COFFEE HOUSE PRESS books are available to the trade through our primary distributor, Consortium Book Sales & Distribution, 1045 Westgate Drive, Saint Paul, MN 55114. For personal orders, catalogs, or other information, write to: Coffee House Press, 27 North Fourth Street, Suite 400, Minneapolis, MN 55401.

LIBRARY OF CONGRESS CIP INFORMATION
Nowak, Mark, 1964–
      Revenants / Mark Nowak
          p. cm.
      ISBN 1-56689-107-8 (alk. paper)
          I. Polish Americans--Poetry. 2. Buffalo (N.Y.)--
Poetry. I Title.
      PS3564.O9366 R48 2000
      811´.6 —— DC21   00-043098

                                           CIP

10 9 8 7 6 5 4 3 2 1

PRINTED IN THE UNITED STATES

Contents

this book is dedicated
to Harry R. Nowak,

1937-1999

The author would like to thank the editors of the following broadsides, journals, and anthologies in which some of these poems first appeared: ACM *(Another Chicago Magazine), The Alembic, American Anthropologist, An Anthology of New (American) Poets, Backwoods Broadsides Chaplet Series, Berkeley Poetry Review, Chariton Review, Children of the Cold War: A Scrapbook, Deskryptions of an Imaginary Universcity, Disturbed Guillotine, First Intensity, Five Fingers Review, Giants Play Well in the Drizzle, Hamline Journal, House Organ, hummingbird, Lightning & Ash, The Little Magazine, Longhouse, lyric&, The Midwest Quarterly, Northwest Review, Puerto del Sol, The Raven Chronicles, Talisman, Working Title: Intercultural Studies,* and *Xcp: Cross-Cultural Poetics.*

The Pain-Dance Begins

It is

an intricate dance

to turn & say goodbye

to the hills we live in the presence of .

When mind dies of its time

it is not the place goes away   .

——PAUL BLACKBURN

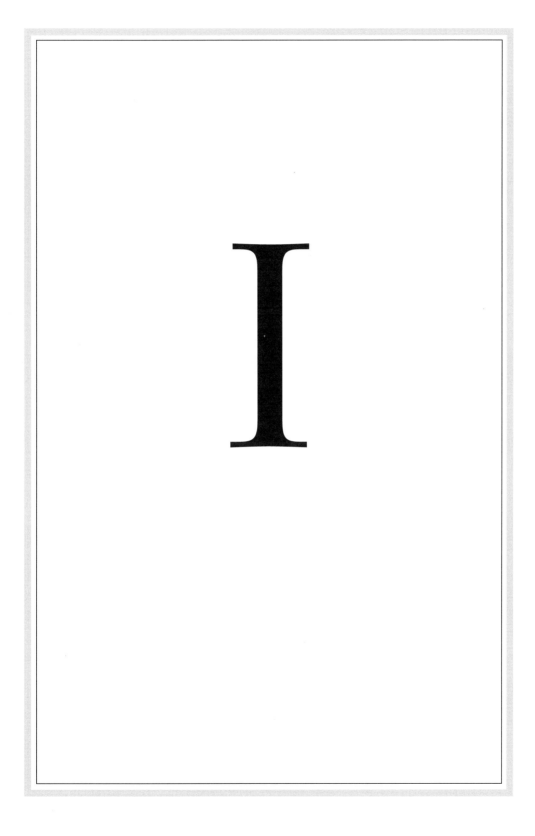

I

Worn shoes in the days of my youth
now have hung the bear.
                              The boys I knew
(Kujowski, Michalski, Czechowski . . .

               follow the sledge
lamenting the Shrovetide Bear.

His neck will be stuffed
with fresh black pudding

and his shoes will be enormous,

for we have worn ours, *skutek,* have
for the magnificent years of our youth
gone through more than our share.

And for this the Shrovetide Bear
(and not the boys I knew . . .
will be taken to the gallows.

Under a Norway Spruce
               (in Transylvania at the end of
the Carnival . . .

two girls crowned with evergreen
(for they have not worn out their shoes)
the sentence they will pronounce
will be the death of the Bear.

And the boys I knew, they
just go to the plaza, they

just buy themselves new shoes.

On the day on which it took place,
two hundred years ago or present-day Lithuania,
                (time is that way . . .
"So take a bite of iron," he said, "It will render
                harmless
the spirit that's in the corn."   Except today,
   zwyczaj, your teeth aren't that strong,

even the thought of it makes your teeth feel weak.

"You slice your bread so thin," he said, thinking
   I was really making sure there wasn't
anyone inside. "And it's so white, your bread.
   Whatever happened to all the grains?"

           So it's bleached wheat,
so I don't want to bite the iron, so I tell the man
from Lithuania, "You're nothing but a savage."

   But the next morning, or at some point
within the next few hundred years (time is that way . . .
   bread may rise in ovens built for
other purposes, perhaps in Lithuania. It will rise,

it will not be white, it will have a myth told about it.

   On the day on which this takes place,
zwyczaj, I have no doubt   you'll be born again.

Stworzenie

You must not whisper these words in the darkness. These words
these. You must not whisper them.

                                    So began the world. In the darkness
so began the world. The world began this way. It began with these words.

You must not you mustn't no.

The gods they said do anything but don't do that. Said that to kids just born.
They knew they would. Said you must not you mustn't no and knew they would.

What a way for gods to start the world.

Would think they could do better than that. Would think they could forgive.

But they didn't, and these words these
nobody wants you to know.

Forget your cosmogonies, your
green-glass bottles filled with
                                    toenails.
lilac petals.
yeast.
            Civilizations
"it's been said" must write
their history, *wzorek,*

for without this alphabetic word
it would be
                        impossible

to drag some former families
into the present,
                        especially when
their past in this place

does not quite belong.
(It is unsettling . . .

The very first crossing of the sea
meant that the newspapers would say,

"A child is born
beneath a single star."

And then the clerics . . .

And then the clergymen . . .

Then decrees from the Pope . . .

I mean, I want to tell my story
straight,

except that's not how
my hair grows, & will never be

the sun's journey across the sky.

Wzorek, there's still the Virgin Mary
glued to the dashboard of your car.

There's sausages smoked in steel drums.
the slaughterhouse.
     an East Side backyard.

Can't we name it all where the world
emerged? Or worlds,
if we're taking any of this seriously.

Struggling to be the sun again,
these few words I have
            (may they remain . . .
a calendar, a tool.

Piper from the village of Sopotnia.

Mirzec woman in festival costume.

Would the days bring you together
how this English book does,
                    facing each other
on the opposite page?

Samotnik, you could be the name
of a vodka they sell in America.
                        You could
be the timber of the house behind

that woman's face.

See her, how the sunrise catches her,
clouds pass between them and shade
her left cheek and eye.
                    But then that's
a relative darkness when you're
speaking of a Pole.

"A Polack in school?" they used to say.

For this the old ones gathered at the market
    (in the stories it's been told . . .
Onions in tin ladles. Butter on a cast-
iron pan.
            Envelopes with locks of hair:
Nowicki, Barus, Michalski, Nowak . . .
none of them golden.

Bowls filled with non-blue eyes.

Zwiastowanie

"I am a goat browsing in the corn."
"I am St. Casimir blessing owls in the trees."

    (We speak of identity w/ split tongues . . .

"I am fertilizer pouring from a wound in my side."
"I am sewing sheep-costumes for the wolves."

"I am St. Casimir cooking fish on a kerosene stove."

"I am wearing a bird-skin parka."
"I am St. Casimir in black wooden shoes."

"I am the head of a goat on the street-lamp in front of your house."

    (Even the saints forget themselves . . .

"I am from the village of Gorzeń Dolny."
"I am the hornets' nest in your left ear."

"I am St. Casimir, goddamnit. Look at these goat-skin shoes."

    (Listen, freak, tell me who the fuck you are . . .

"I am the corn and nothing but the corn. So help me god."

"I am the mile you walked back to your name."

The sun rises each morning simply because I am separated from the sun.
                        If there were a way for me to
tie a string to it, ride its path at a comfortable distance from its rays,

then I might not need to enter my house in the morning.
then I might never have to leave my house again.

To reach Pittsburgh by six o'clock in the morning, *droga*, the sun doesn't plan.
Nor does it project to arrive in the Pacific Northwest around six a.m.

Dawn, like sound, is evanescent. It is like a struck gong that is going
out of existence. It disappears itself into the light of my morning.

If there was just a story for this, a young girl who slept so long she finally went
blind, and in her complete night she was able to tell us how the sun won't rise,

how it's we who step from our sleep to notice it again.

It was perhaps explained by a custom. That in seeing a certain thing
as cause (iron ploughshares, improper disposal of cut nails . . .

   another thing is said to happen (dry weather, war . . .

And this event, attributed, & called a vision "by the one who sits . . ."

I have sat & sat, *oko,* made a map
of where I planned to be
in a dozen years, an hour from now,
that second just passed.

          Place, as term: what good is it to think "Mille Lacs"
& not know where it is?

I have seen you, *oko,* in the history
of society, traced our origins back to you. From that early time,
what happens, as cause, makes the moment local (so they go back
to the wooden ones for a year . . .

And this event becomes a certain thing,
it passes into common use, & lore.

We bear this knowledge. And it is
vexatious to the later Christian church.

That a northern territory of slain animals
(who dreamt Old Father girt into their skins . . .

      is un-dead, partly
      & exploited

for the tourists
   of a more determinate clock. Watch,
markotno, for his black flaxen beard
& the dead horse.
                His hat, you know,
the horns they have their roots on the inside.

Take the money-box where the son encounters
who he may become.

"For the horse must be buried," he says.
                  And this brings
them out, *markotno,* the ones with coins to spare.

Pale men in blue suits with baskets attached
to sticks; they reach their arms across all
religions for this one.
                I knew that well, asked
my father when the box is full, what then?
                   "Look into
the box," Old Father says.

      Blueberries & radishes
      where the coins had been.

Still   it is you,
     tutaj,

         in the space
my want claims.

Awakened

& the presence of
     awake.

If there is no quiet
in either of these

we must choose one,

     it's what we've been
placed
in the world for.
         How
in the morning it's
the anotherness
        that pleases us,

(which of course we lose
throughout the day . . .

     Yet we wake,
         again
& again to the all of you,
     tutaj.

That the gods keep
         giving you
until they take you away.

But let's not talk about
such certainties.
        Yes, it's there
around the corner,
but so is the kitchen.

  Let's look:

awakened & the presence
of awake.
        (And where did
the quiet go, did it
move to?)
          Let's look at
the thin line that separates
  the doorway
from the door.

Let's look at how
our first footstep
rooms the world.

Our concept of this field, of objects and their positions
relative to a certain fixed point, & Adam & Eve, they come down
from the Garden of Eden.

This is resolved by myths, by an expansion
that is not the same as made the village. But was the world requires not the premise,

nor its customs or beginnings, all drawn against the necessity of certain hours?

(The three great monotheistic religions
share the nomadic background of their earliest source,
they share the moon . . .

From the same unmarked place here, generation after generation,
there was nothing designed, only the local occurrences and the flight.

(And the medicine of chance events,
& the goats were able to be herded . . .

Until we separate out, to Hebel &Tubal-
Cain, & the smith overturned the ground: (w/o a history) the soil is a borrowed phrase.

A story built, *żniwo*, like the wall without due reverence to the gods,
and for nine days space was drave their flood,
and the battlefield disappeared in the sand.

So that you might be praised, *okruch,* as a brother must be praised.

Even when the brother wrongs, or is wronged, or the conception of something
   incorrect may be said to pass through his consciousness.

An elm-oak wood, *okruch,* and you are found under that table.

I wanted to stop, to say I was something other than the one perceived, to speak,
   speak in my own tongue of the communion that exception offers.

An iron skillet, *okruch,* except you have escaped that fire.

Because a synonym for except happens to be save.

As the world knows, no?

Grzech Pierworodny

A painting of the Garden of Eden
(found in Kołaczyce, Poland . . .
            in which everything is red.
The apples.
The tongue of a jackal.
A rooster's plume.
                    Even the rooster's
legs are red, the rooster's feet
      & the jackal's tongue
poised next to Adam's left leg.

One unicorn, one snail,
            one snake is winding up
the apple tree with apples
                        (they are only
half red . . .
            Adam's tongue, in his
red mouth: red. Eve's tongue is red.

      Three hills behind two chalices.
      One shovel that I think is a tree.

                    But who this father
that didn't want us
to know, Who made taking
what's red
            (become . . .
awareness, difference & banishment
in our very first story?

So much for red. So much
for having red.

Whatever the creation is, *oczekiwać,* behind it lies a form that we must sign.

That we must form a single line behind whatever the creation states.

Minus the light toward it.

At the gate and then locate the world.

I do not know, *oczekiwać,* how the sun presses against us.

Nor do I have the throat to write that song.

Woda, first you were a dog
following that river.
             The plan is complex.

Masks were worn. A small head
and a rather obtrusive belly.

You got the reputation, *Woda,*
of being that belly-mask.

And so now when you're hungry
that damn belly growls like a dog.

One woman she walked along
                 that river.
Her name was *Woda.*

First woman ever to walk
alone like that.
             But then the frozen river
cracked, water welled over.

No one knows
whatever happened to her.

Someone, *Woda,* named Jesus said,
"Salmon—bigger than your car—

would swim upstream so thick
that I could walk out on the water."

Where is that river? Ask the man
who built the Hoover Dam.

★

Woda, I'll name you bottles.

I'll name you re-tread tires & red balloons.

　　All you've got to do
is turn the faucet on, *Woda,* and out run
kidney beans.
amulets. perfume.

Everything, *Woda,* will run out.

Everything.

Cast it into the sea,

                    allow for it the world again,

about to fall among other stories . . .

                             the saltwater

you have lived your life owing to.

                     Ulewa,

toward Hera's imitation of childbirth,

          through her robes, toward earth,

speaking your name.

The King of Scotland has this affection for you, *piosenka,*
as does the Duke of Normandy, father of William I.

  Even a British field marshal and a French lawyer
and revolutionary. They love you, you, *piosenka,* on and
off the continent.

And it may be that the blue or the red of you reminds them
of another.   Or it may be that the blue or red of you
reminds them of themselves.

Either way, it suggests a center, a place to return. And you
return, *piosenka,* as the vertical self returns.
                              As the forsythia do, as
asparagus does, early.
                    But we're too busy for you, or, if we do
notice, we get caught up in defining you as birth, as re-birth,
or that the early bird gets the worm.

To this tired polis you have returned, *piosenka,* and if you
come in, come inside.
                    But who am I asking, you? You who have
returned, again, again, on and on to this city.

As is proper for such people, *piosenka,* I have spoke little,
and heard even less.   Certainly I greet you, I ask you
inside.
                    But there is where it ends, at the third
repetition as it has ended before, is where and when the out-
side gets in and I hear you, *piosenka, piosenka, piosenka.*

And if one could mix these things, *ziemniak,* even if one could afford them at market.

        The representation, in space, is the all of you. I would kiss you if I could find you, I would eat you raw at the beginning of the war, *ziemniak,* sweet or red.

        For many years is a question of location, of whether you are calling all around you silence or sound.

        Your name is like gardenias, is the color of gardenias are. In the yard, in the backyard, if only you.

And in Poland in the sheaf
last bound

        sits Old Woman.

And *Baba* gets a ride home
on the last harvest wagon.

And she is given to those who
spent their season attending her.

And to the woman last to bind
is found with child next year.

And her body is the sheaf
& only her face is human.

And she is carried to the well
& waters are poured upon her.

And she remains the sheaf
& next year

        is born to her
laughter.

Light with these the entrance among them, who began to rule
my house. (We can cross and exchange . . .

                                                        In a few minutes,
several years ago, near the bottom is a small time-piece,
a reference to light, when the sun is carried in a basket back from
the horizon.

                        What is this place we consider decisive, *obliczać czas,*
that question dips behind and rises from.
that carries us through.
that "now".

                                        I became for the first my house inside of this,
and not knowing tied a string to the rest of the world.

II

Next to an elk's club next to
the market that sold
        spices and yarns (becoming . . .
what a place at which to awaken.

Not merely mother and farther
the borning of "me"
            but an entire cosmology
of stars (this was my grandmother's name,
her posture.

the fire of her blood.

Whose feasts, whose religions?
The elder men hunched over
their wives unable
to outlive them.

Father and matter in a room
painted white (the tall one
always hid in the ceilings of
houses we emigrated from . . .
            "Others" of these
(The subject being a slip in one
alphabet for mother?

        nowiutki   :   brand-new
          walać   :   soil, stain

there was a rug on the floor.

fan-blown furnace corners one
of the rooms, it's blowing away.

My grandmother, she arrived
with hand-crocheted robes:

"I remember your name."

Carnivals, festivals,
novenas to the Black Madonna
at the church where we
prayed on our knees.
                              Strings
of sausages, strings of beads.

        walać : soil
     lamować : border

Near the cascades where
how many families had
saved each other's lives?

how many lost them?
                         Religions, white
waters in this river, sheephead,
sheep herders, their bare woolen coats.

Cots set up outside in the hospital wing,
an owl.
                My grandmother, my "star"
my gold wedding ring if only she was
                         back again
I'd wear a ring of iron in that place.

The first of November, now then, *nowiutki:*
            pumpkins, apples, and pears.

That market I was born on the block of
            sells curry and marjoram leaves.
               These, the former,
some of them have crossed the world. It was
                         difficult
for some of the families to cross the river here.

Many of them died among white waters. My
grandmother, I was told, and the moon rises
            in the Carpathian Mountains.

                                    Rises.

            A place at which to begin.

A friend of mine (she is blind . . .
            she tells me of her old home
in northern Rumania.
                        We speak
of the mountains there, a spine that connects
her house and mine.

                        I think about
St. Casimir feeding birds. I think
about the Infant of Prague.

"What you will see,
when you ride those rivers
from Bosnia-Hercegovina
to the Black Sea,"
                        she says,
"It is a miracle."

nowy	:	new
nowo urodzony	:	newborn
noworoczny	:	New Year's Day

One falling, the old man begins again, these hands a few clouds
in the winter sky.
                       You may not recognize, you may not always be
able to afford this vision of the world my prayer begins.

The sun, the porcelain basin that the sun warms, my grandfather,
many of the rise, *jutro,*
many of them.

"So the bishop slapped you on the face. So you took my name."

"Will you remember at your Christmas table to set me a place?"

My grandfather never straightened himself again:
                                  water poured from
the porcelain basin to however it returns to the sea.

The sun, each place it is all around me and quite difficult to obtain
a sense I'd ever known this person.
      That clouds, that this winter sky, *jutro,* that any of it
waits, belongs, is other than dark and more intangible

than how the clay is packed in a certain mud and fired.
than how that falling that day an old man who might have been
      my grandfather
took the stairs and so pardoned himself to the sky.

The calendar of you, *zboże,* yield of Demeter, and the moon, the North Star,
        these also are songs.
                When it is understood that to renew the objects
(a hawk, bluebirds, a bear . . .

these narratives used by the one who seeks are supposed to have songs of their own.

        I would suppose, *zboże,* that the house the plow broke the prairie for
        had not these hymns at heart; and yet the grass is pregnant with you.

The calendar, the yield of Demeter, the moon, and the North Star. A hawk,
bluebirds, and a bear.
        I learn the prairie not by the mouthing of these names,
nor any others. Not even the songs I've learned will save me here.

Nebraska, a tune my throat caught. Iowa, a drum that nobody's tuned.

Minnesota, a river so dark that even the fires won't touch it.

The winter is gathered, as are we, and only the first foot of you, *zboże,* is
still left standing on this earth.
            And then the snows come to cover you.
            And then the earth is laid upon our graves.
            And time, it is still the origin of time.

But as when dogs & country-folk pursue a goat
that sits himself in the corn, then the blue-flowers

                                        in this landscape

put your ear against gold.

          Allotted, this is the last
          handful, *wszyscy na raz,*

          it will bear a whole year.

This is the day who brings home, is believed to be the slower reaper
wreathed in each hour.
                    When the wind bends the corn, we say,
"The Goat is browsing there."

"The wind is driving the Goat through the corn."

The field becomes this day when the dogs & country-folk pursue
much more than you, Goat, sitting or browsing through the corn.

          But in saying that the field must bear another, another,
we have seen blue-flowers gone gold, have seen farmhouse sow another,
larger out-building, have even questioned, "Is there another?"

In this landscape,
in this windswept,
in this (our . . .

          Allotted, this is the last
          handful, *wszyscy na raz,*

          it will bear a year, entire.

We have now observed that the practice of agriculture
        could explain certain things,
    the notion that we can transfer guilt & suffering is
        familiar to our spirit.
Yet when it arises between the materials: scythes, barley,
    stones . . . it is then that the world
acts, from our refinements & theology, to bear upon
        the castoffs
    we see as falling to Hell, them all.

And birds, they with their din expand the field, whose cheep
does rid their need of *sprawdzić*. To them their gods
they are the winds, the castoffs from Heaven.
"They are the owl (of ill omen) that hoots in the town."
And that it is the world who sets the boundaries for them,
        for they

would wish the world instead to give rise, and the thunders
        surge
across the farmhouse. They adore those gardens, over
the gate, through a hole in the fence always made just for them.
Beside the creek the owl sets its claws upon two snakes.
That brought rain, brought by an access to wind.

These (Terra, Aqua, Ignis, Aer) could not mimic the world, the wife
with child, the farmer smiles at a storm gathering, he looks up
and believes the same befalls his in-laws,
believes this to be more than a local occurrence: it is this daze
        that traces on the heels of humanity.

Zdarzenie, what if the breath anyone is about
to breathe is
not here?
        A child bell-caster, in from the provinces,
watches a man in blue swim trunks he might have been
   many years from now, in a specific location,

some distance south of the waters of Hudson Bay.

By the same token that Adam is not a man (in Hebrew . . .
the moon shines
            half-way around the world,
a walleye hits a Red Devil spoon in the waters of Lake Mille Lacs.

Zdarzenie, not unlike the one that swims, the one that watches,

(the poem just stops as a hummingbird takes its fill of nectar . . .

one attempts to explain the lake in a high school biology class.
A blue heron, the shout of the man in blue swim trunks,
"Throw it over here," bark unfurling from a birch . . .

How is anyone to know which of these the breath, which
the air we breathe?
        So many boats, so many cries of children
playing in the water.

For the quilt-maker to have no religion
because she has religion.

                              For the three sisters
to work the earth well: wind, an ear, the dance.

Someone's house (it was built in 1905 . . .

I walked through it today.

Asking for a name, not the price or yield,
but how one such as me
                        a bell-caster,
"a bald-headed white boy" with a long beard

is expected to wait patiently while the hour
leverages against me,
                        pulls in this direction
for that.
               Infinite, infinite, *zapalić się*,

take the earth that is cast about me and cast me
anew.
        Praise, ask forgiveness and not too many
questions.
               Accept the hour because
no other can the mind consume.

A long beard, the one, the other she wears
a thimble on her finger.
                        Waits for it,
there above the neighborhood at noon.

Okulary

The goddess of the black fire, behind the window my grandfather's eyes
are sensitive to noise. He whispers novenas to the black goddess, he wears
glasses in all the photographs and grimaces. Only to her he confides.

She is undying for him. He is sensitive to noise. Arms wait behind
the houses, a door closing or a barking dog. The goddess of the black fire
is more than a shadow in his thought. My grandfather looks out the window.

We did not move southeast of San Antonio. We did not move to rural Illinois.
The black goddess of the fire listens to his whispered novenas. He believes
that she is undying. In all the photographs my grandfather is grimacing.

He wears glasses because his eyes are sensitive to noise. A dog barking
might be arms right before the key enters the door. Even the refrigerator is
humming too long. The black goddess, the woman that he whispers to.

Crooked arms, crooked canes that she leans on,
Great Bear in the northwest sky.
         Curled back her birds,
leans on her back shawl their wings.

In the distance the elevator silo the tracks
maybe of a train. Little Dipper
  in the northern sky. An azure that opens
to her companions opens to her
elbows, *również:*

she is the stretches that time her, their rings.

Talk of witches if you will, eithers that make her
pagan or sane.
  Did I mention she walks with a cane?

Expect the fox at her ankles, the one who
haunts her, outwits a crow bearing cheese.
  At three-thirteenths moon
up from the river watch him creak in his bones:

he comes bearing burdock with Mars
off toward Bismarck, North Dakota.

Craned neck, craned like the water
-animal she's borrowing it from.
         Slightly
dark, only, like the very under
-side of her wings.

Craned, crooked, craned:
how *Baba Jaga* first got named.

My throat the world caught like trees.

Hewn, the word is hewn, pronounced hewn.

Close your eyes you can hear the moon grow larger.

Shut the thunder off like a hose.

Krawcowa, if only against and together.

She wore that dress in the rain.

Not the river that he wanted her to become.

This wind-swept *zboże,* sown forth in expanse
      in a holy place.
Was to behold the evening (yellow-red & reaching . . .
      stretching out below the sky.

The Ukraine priest did bless, the Russian priest himself is rolled,
by women, "Without regard to the mud & holes he may encounter
      in his beneficent progress."
In the house you are (as wolf or dog or ox that the wind sets in there . . .
was built a second, more stable structure, that fears this other home.
      From here, the *zboże*
it did spring forth & swept the nation clear across,
      between the mouths of the two rivers.

On the day the seed breaks ground, go tell the married couples.
Go tell the old wives & the widows. It is into them that the expanse
      has lain the spell of the earth.

Ram and deer are cake figures
from the Ostrołęka District.
              Who shares
the tilled soil shares
their beneficent aspect.

Ram cake, deer cake, song sung
through the throat.

Babka is a round cake because the
old woman's dress was round,
              wore it when she made
that reindeer cake.

Bells jangle the dress she wears
she sewed eggshells on her cape.
              (Each time the doll is
opened, another, inside, appears . . .

  1 quart scalded milk
  2 dry yeast, 6 eggs
  $^{1}/_{2}$ lb. butter, sugar, raisins,
     flour & salt

Don't forget she was a mid-wife,
grandmother.
              Don't forget to add
one seed of rye.

Don't forget "to let it bake for a while."

In Ostrołęka, some say that ram
              got drunk on sweet Hungarian wine.
              Some say,
"Reindeer, keep yourself
out of those fields."

Or *Babka* just might bake you.

Straszak

cast into
the firepit.

"He'll get
religion

from this."
Women

look for
cups of

rain. Men
order flame

-proof
clothes.

Oczekiwanie

A straw effigy of death, with puppets about to bury you in the water. Go to the rivers
Warta and Vistula where my people awaited you,

and bury the puppets that carried you

to these streams. A beech branch fastened with an apple for a head will do.

Polish girls that swaddle potatoes in dolls' clothes to keep them from the Russians,
carry your dolls to the Warta and Vistula, and bury them in the sand.

For it is night that grows these eyes, daylight when ravens wait in the trees above them.

Expecting it to happen. Expecting the knuckles of a hand to three times
knock against your door.

        Not staying awake each night in case it might happen.

Nevertheless, it wouldn't surprise you if it did.

You know you don't belong, really, wherever you happen to be reading this now.

        And yet your shirt seems to fit, and if you went to the mirror
your hair would most likely be the color it was the morning before.

So why the wait, *pytanie,* why the chewing on fingernails and the tapping
of a hand against my leg, a hand that all these years I thought was mine.

Winter and early spring I want you back again,
I am one of the old men in disguises
      who roam the Polish countryside.
Dressed in sheepskin and horns, leading
into the village   a bear on a string:

it replenishes. You say fear, *rozum,*
I brought to your house, I frightened your entire
family. Any more than walking the streets now?
Any more than never really knowing where
what you ate this morning was born?

This morning was born: thirty-seven thousand
chickens, six hundred and forty-three cows,
one million nine hundred eighty-five
thousand two hundred and seventeen garlic cloves.

You say I'm breathing on you, *rozum,* my
breath is bad. You say,
      "Get yourself some Listerine."

The catches of this world are that it
nourishes   nearly or not at all.
Those fruit juices at the market, for example:
less than two percent Vitamin C.

How did we do it? How did we ever imagine
that we could chase the Krakówian, that beggar,
out into the streets and he wouldn't come back
  to haunt us?

The first snow is a begins, *warstwa,* is a brought down of what
leaves brought down, a falling is.
                              Where, always where the grade
lies acute, the first snow that is, how is it said to have clung.

                    Let the sky again, begin again, again.

It holds, a part of it does. Because beneath what falls is a history
of falling, it is what is ground, all that does not hold, which is all.

Not to worry, *warstwa,* the moon tonight and to see the cup
is to know the cup is empty, tonight. And after tonight?

What is there from what we believe to be falling to keep us from?

In the northern range in the mountains, "neighborhood" it is called
their starting place.
                              Often the sun rises very red the sun crosses
the horizon. At harvest time the corn like the women and men
                    return
to their houses. As the dry ears are laid to be stored
through the season when the fields lie barren,
                                        this is the time
                                        this is the evidence
of the time when one travels to the cemeteries and addresses
the Lord of the Dead.
                              And the contrast of this life of ours on this earth,
skrzyżowanie,
the surface of this earth in contrast to the Underworld to the sky.

Without the earth for him or her to walk across, the day, year . . .
                    returns (even in
                    these mountains)
the dimensions of the house to the cyclical paths of the sun.

moje świadectwo:

Northern fields, a half-
dozen pears, one yellow jacket
caught between
the storm window and the storm.

The sunlight is over

and over again.

III

How shall I praise you, polis, as the center or
the snare at the center?

        Either of you is not an eye, is why
so often you are
    at the mouth of a river. You are a saying,
polis, and a devouring.

Or so it got put by one *teoria,* which has little
to do with diamonds or the southwest side of
Chicago.
        But perhaps a bit, for when we
go there, we go there to stay,
    by which we mean simply that it is a good
place to have sausages.

I wonder if Wittgenstein ate sausages.

To beg the question, how shall I praise you, what
can I say about you
                that you don't proclaim
on your own. You are a gatherer of bodies, of
the very youngest and the very oldest of bodies,

which you devour. But what about Heidegger,

does he eat sausages? So you are a mouth, poetry
has found a way to you, but already you're off
propagandizing,
                  aware
of the correct pronunciation of "welcome" in
forty-seven languages.

But did you know, *teoria,* did you know, polis,

that there are tongues that refuse your words,

        there are mouths and gums, lips,
in which to say welcome means "what has
gone wrong
for you?"

The house or hand that forces an American into you.
The approaching arms the approaching horizon arrive.

The approaching horizon that opens out over the prairie.
Arrives at the house and forces open the door.

He would open the door for the equivalent of a dollar.
George Washington lived without ever opening the door.

The hand that signed the Declaration of Independence.
The house at which the approaching horizon arrives.

Thomas Jefferson never visited the prairie.
He arrives at his house and imagines opening the door.

Approaching arms the book he wrote before you.
Before you, *grób*, Jefferson and Washington arrive.

Arrive with arms that are pointed toward the prairie.
Arrive with arms that forced you open before.

Nearly gone nearly everyone from the neighborhood.

Almost as if, or if, an edict had been drawn.

Had been or about to have been handed down.

The trespasser, *nie nazwany,* the trespasser.

Yards where tomatoes rot, and cabbage rots.

Each nearly empty, or as if to be silenced.

Nie nazwany, the interpreter or interpreted.

Naming each that has vacated the premises.

Each hand a tomato or edict hand.

That it might even become known as the cultivated.

That the neighborhood might even become known.

Had been a mirror of a former gathering.

Except escaped here.

Escaped to be named the trespasser.

To be drawn down to the vacated premises.

To see a former house, silenced.

Each room a manifestation of a decade.

One room in particular where the sheets were drawn.

Where a body might be lain in this silence.

The body known as *nie nazwany.*

Where known suggests a similar cultivation.

Yards where tomatoes rot, potatoes lie unearthed.

In a cavity where they might have been planted.

Almost as if an edict had been drawn.

An edict forbidding the growth of potatoes

Potatoes seen as reflections of former gatherings.

One room in particular where potatoes had been washed.

Where potatoes were washed and peeled.

Even washing and peeling have ceased.

In a room like any other.

Except as a manifestation of this scene.

This scene where a body might be lain.

The body known as *nie nazwany.*

Which cannot be translated as.

Which cannot be translated until.

A crow caws in a tree, and not only is the speech of the crow inscrutable: so is the tree.

This and other "truths" remained suspect to an age that believed all things were decipherable.

To you, age, I say *żałować*. *Załować,* in the name of the . . .

Although I mean it, and project it to the vertical (by which
I do not mean northern, *stacja*—)
    I have no children or turnips to return to, and what home
now means is not worth the fare.

The kitchen is an interrogative sentence, is empty.

So I am writing this novel out of character. So I am a husband
who raises cattle. So I live in an apartment. So I raise a question.

    I have no cabbage, no cats to come home to, *stacja,*
so I sit with you, the newspaper and cigarette of you.

The kitchen is a sentence, is.

I do believe it, which is why I repeat it, if by repetition we
mean how history rhymes, and how the rhyme changes.
                        If we mean that "tall" rhymes
with "soul," this may represent an earlier time.

                Time when it was (the pronoun rhymes
the kitchen here) centered at the hearth (rhyming earth,
rhyming vertically at birth and built).

So I am writing this novel in the bathroom. So I am writing this novel
in your attic. So I cannot complete a sentence. I begin so I cannot.

The kitchen, *stacja,* I return through you, and am you.

Think of it, *charakter pisma,* pressed beads pressed in the palm over an
epoch leave no mark, no etched impress across the fingers they crossed.

A like practice that was not phenomenological, not concerned with practical questions.

Scripted, because the house is the box the palm is the leave of salvation.

An order that distinguishes the apple from the light
in which the apple appears.

Here, where the circle meets the square, are you, *dworzec,*
the very cut of you, like the four sides of a sonata.

Here, where the teasel reaches the driveway is you, even
if you were to deny it, *dworzec,* broken-glass one.

For years, from the birth to death of children in years,
the way we as a people count them and keep counting

them is you. Here, where our inquiries are stopped by
fence and chain, where even our eyes have shut themselves

to your leaving is you, *dworzec,* sow-carrier and coal-
hearted-stoker, gone-one. Like the four sides of a sonata,

some wrought with pastiche, others with boundless
energy or melodrama, like these four inalienable sides,

dworzec, you have come into the world, my world, into
the heart of it, you, cleft-leaver and time signature.

Most of us live beyond the shadow of you, *powoli,* an inch farther than
your arm could reach if it needed to.

Because to speak your name
is to say it at dawn, or sometime when the sun is reaching or just has reached

the beginning of the sky. But there's a basket at the other end, we're told, and
it's not our own.

And yet we want what's there, so we stretch our hand
beyond the edge of the table because we've heard there's some better fruit
to be had.

And we have been.

Off-shore,
even if there was
a shore,
   some
distance from it.

To forget
what comes next,
odzew,
   what
the wind sweeps
across the water,

even if there was.

To give name to what
we cannot grasp
theoretically.

What we cannot grasp,

believe it or not, we cannot
lay hold
of all things

and make them theorems.

     So you are
surprised, *odzew,*
casting out below the bridge
 where the river empties
to the bay,

even if there was
a bridge or river.

"There was a river,"
you whisper to a child,
except, except . . .

Things happened,
unnameable things,
happened.
        The fish, well,
there were fish in the river.

Now there are none.

        There was
a beauty in the way this
river was described
by the townspeople who were,
by and large,
dependent upon the river.

But now?

Now it is forbidden
to even mention the former
tributaries of this river.

Of course,
of course in out-buildings
(and behind the firehouse)
has spread a mythology,
    which has grown,
grown in relation to
the disappearance of the river,

so that now, why,
one would almost think

that it still flowed
out into the bay.

One might still be deceived
into believing,
    yes, believing that a boy
could walk the dirt road
out of town,
                and return
(as evening settled upon
the elms and porches . . .

with a basket of fish.

But if this did, in fact,
happen.
            If a boy walked
down the dirt road and
over the bridge
with a basket of fish,

what would we say?

Would we believe, *odzew,*
that it was time again
for music and dancing?

    Or would we
assume the boy a thief,
jail him,

and continue to interpret
our mythology?

The river and the sky, *odwrotny*, . . . and the sky . . .

On the other side is as much as suffices.

The same there and the rest of these things.

You are yellow, *ranek,* in your backyard behind vines. You
are yellow as squash is, or beans.

        It is the color of importance, yellow, you can see it in
a house, when the window frames are black.

                        You are yellow, you are, *ranek,* and
nothing you can grow denies it. Nothing you can plant
behind a row of sunflower, or to the rear in back of the corn.

A mother in a dress, *ranek,* and you are in her eyes.

You are yellow, you, your shape is, without understanding it
even your gestures are.

        And it is the color of a hand, *ranek,* this yellow is,
at the very end of the harvest.

Na Około,
Na Około,

even at the stove or shower
    I am deep in
Gods.

"Now carry we Death out of
            the village."

Cook some corn & beans.

Take a bath.

Na Około.

Lights in the bushes it could be
birds
    except it's Christian time, Christmas
time again it's that
                which denies them.

Temple now that the leaves have
disappeared their traces,
erased the trees.
              I could walk out
in the twenty-below weather
with clay pots of split peas, cashews.

Build a fire for another species
that might be born tomorrow.

An older man in brown sweater
and pants pale blue
              laid the electric
cord across the tops of their faces.

I was drinking orange pekoe tea
in a Chinese mug with a blue
carp painted on.
              These colors,
on the outside, have dispersed.

Another neighbor will fill his yard
with green spot-lights and
gingerbread deer,
              another will tape
the jolly old boy to her door.

Folk customs purchased at K-Mart,
      wróżba, that breathe
through the seams still holding
it all in place.

The ploughed field was visible across the river. But that was another time, another time. In the morning you could see the field, *potomek*, but that was definitely another time, yes. Now the field is an abandoned factory, and the river, well even an old man wouldn't recognize himself there, an old man would look at his hands and say, "Who's there?"

Fog driving through houses where I
bent to my knees—
       all I had taken with me
disperses from my knapsack like a
ink pen breaking in my hands.

in my hands.

Totally aware that it's a lamp
that lights this room
           completely
(they're beginning the announcements . . .

 "And the same thing happens
"To Teddy Krystyniak . . .
"To Bronislaw Malinowski . . .
"To Paderewski Drive . . .

Red blankets, white pillow cases,
oak tables opening to the birds.

Wake to the light on, *niżej,*
and into another dream:

water has been running into and from
the kitchen sink for hours,
      and a last handful of 2% milk
(if one could hold such things . . .
has just this moment gone bad.

Through the spaces comes it all, its
own way—
      whatever you thought
to grab:
house, car, brother . . .

you'll never have.

The world will turn, sunflowers will rise against the horizon, and fish,
they'll continue to be caught.

                     Clocks, they tick the same in a small town
(not more than twenty miles from the border of Czechoslovakia . . .

except the calendar is taped to a rock instead of the fridge. This is not a
sentence because I said it in the basement: you're nothing but a chicken.

Zakończenie, what will I brave to walk these cities' streets again, when
the wind is blowing through the empty rooms through the houses that are
no longer filled with frying onions or your future.

                            This is a sentence if this
is the way of the world. The line turned as the world does, and to speak
what's here on this page the reader has to breathe. Is that enough?

Someone looks here to the book to find what the world has not held
long enough for him or her to experience.

                   And so one is here,
zakończenie, writing, so that another one day might read.

                           This is a sentence.
I say it out loud, I breathe it into the world against the horizon line.

Zwyczaj

"Pierogies remind me of Peter Lorre: they're plump, compact, and unglamorous; they thrive in the least promising environments; and wherever they are, be it glamorous Hollywood, decadent Berlin, or a big pile of sour cream, they maintain their essential lumpy, foreign, resilient character."

—CITY PAGES, MINNEAPOLIS
JUNE 11, 1997

1

"With immersion, the field
researcher sees
                from the inside
how people lead their lives
  [zakorzenić się]

how they carry out their
daily rounds of activities
  [zakorzenić się]

what they find
meaningful   *[zakorzenić się]*

and how they do . . ."

For example, the consultant
says:
     "We've got to fix all the roofs,
"the roof's leaking."

A women's group in New York
Mills, New York, is making *pierogi*
in the basement of their church
(where "the roof's leaking")

Someone asks:
How many pierogi
to re-roof
       a heritage?

"I heard that   [my *matka*
says]
     once before."

2

"For them the preparation
"of *pierogi* . . . is an act of religious
"devotion
          "selfless and meritorious."

(When the ethnographer writes
"them," he or she
must locate an ethnographic subject
within . . .

"[My mother] cooked them
in the basement . . .
this way the mess is   always
down there."

What about *this* "them"?
Are cultural "materials" and
cultural "consultants" equal "thems"?

"Immersion in ethnographic research,
then, involves both
being with other people
to see how they respond to events
as they happen
          and experiencing for oneself
these events and the circumstances
that give rise to them."

(Measuring "thems" . . .

3

"In participating as fully and
humanly as possible
in another way of life . . ."

"[My mother] just

**threw everything
together**

and that was it."

       ". . . the ethnographer
learns what is required to become
a member of that world,
    to experience events and
meanings in ways
that approximate
members' experiences."

"These women [of New York Mills]
"display a familiarity with their materials
"that precludes the need
"for measuring cups, cookbooks
"and timers."

(Knowing "them" without measuring . . .

4

"But you
        "don't know

"how hard it was
[Mrs. P. says]

"You come from Poland

"you don't know   "no English
                "and
"you people don't know."

"Moreover, it will often be the case
that relationships with
        those under study follow
political fault lines in the setting,

exposing the ethnographer
                                selectively
to varying priorities
and points of view."
                        **"She just,
I guess, was on, you know,
lived by herself, I guess . . ."**

"You come from Poland . . .

"you don't know . . .

"and you people don't know."

5

"As a result, the task of
the ethnographer
is not to determine   'the truth' . . ."

"**. . . at that time they thought
butter was no good
     so we started frying 'em
in margarine.**"

". . . but to reveal the multiple truths
apparent in others' lives."

"Talking to Mrs. Nogas,
"it becomes clear that being
"a meat packer
   "and an Assistant Pastor's mother
"are not mutually exclusive activities."

6

"... the ethnographer's presence
in a setting
inevitably has implications
for what is taking place."

**"A lot of people
don't like don't put onions in theirs,
and we   put onions in ours.**

        "There are discussions
"and opinions
"on everything

"from current fashions
"to unions."

**That's the way we're used to 'em,
but you know we like onions anyway."**

7

"So I get it to almost
          the final stages
and then [your father] takes it
from there
and he gets the dough nice and
soft, and
    he'll roll it out for me.

"Relationships between
the field researcher
          and people in the setting
do not so much disrupt or alter
ongoing patterns of social interaction
as reveal the terms and bases
on which people form social ties
in the first place."

**So it's like he does the rolling,
and I fill 'em and boil 'em and everything.**

"Mrs. Bielaszka and Mrs. Mikuta
"stand at opposite sides of the basin
"and 'work [the dough] through.'"

**But he does all the fine work
with the dough."**

8

"Rather than detracting from what
the fieldworker can learn . . ."

For example, "The *pierogi* handled
"by each woman are unique in appearance
"due to a variety of individual
"pinching techniques."

". . . first-hand relations with those studied
may provide clues to understanding . . ."

"I   make the half-moon
[my *matka* says]
   & press it down."

These ". . . more subtle, implicit
   underlying assumptions [are]
often not readily accessible
through observation or interview
methods alone."

9

"Many contemporary ethnographers advocate
highly participatory roles
in which the researcher actually
performs the activities
that are central to the lives of those studied."

**"It's just they taste better. And you
get your hands all into 'em
and you accomplish something."**

"It's not just push the button."

10

"Today *pierogi* can be obtained
"in commercial prepackaged form

"but doubtless the   "homemade variety
"available from the women of St. Mary's
"is preferred for Lenten and Christmas meals

"in New York Mills."

**"Oh yeah, there's a lot of people
that buy 'em for Christmas Eve
over there even. They order 'em.**

Instead of making 'em."

". . . close, continuing participation
in the lives of others

                         encourages appreciation
of social life

as constituted by ongoing, fluid processes."

11

"Perhaps   "the family is gone

"but their energy

"and   "sense of responsibility

"remain."

"Through participation, the field researcher
sees first-hand and up-close
how people grapple with uncertainty
and confusion . . ."

"I never really copied any recipe down"

"how meanings emerge through talk
and collective action . . ."
                          **because I don't think
I was interested in it at that time**

"how understandings and interpretations
change over time."
                    **thinking, well, gram
always made 'em and . . . not thinking ahead."**

12

My *matka* still says,

**"I think it's more the people you're with
than it is the food."**

"The women of St. Mary's make
"available to customers   "young and old

"participation in an ethnic tradition

"through the ordinary
"yet unique work

"of cooking."

"In all these ways,
the fieldworker's closeness to others'
daily lives and activities
heightens sensitivity to social life
as process."

NOTE: Boldface quotations in *Zwyczaj* (Polish: custom, practice) are excerpted from transcriptions of ethnographic interviews conducted by the author with Ellen (Michalski) Nowak in May, 1995. All non-boldface quotes are taken from one of two sources: Elizabeth Goldstein and Gail Green's "Pierogi- and Babka-Making at St. Mary's" [*New York Folklore,* vol. 4 (1978): 71-79]; or a section on "Ethnographic Participation" in Robert M. Emerson, Rachel I. Fretz, and Linda L. Shaw's *Writing Ethnographic Fieldnotes* (University of Chicago Press, 1995). The Polish term *zakorzenić się* can be translated as "to get the roots in."

"Back Me Up"

*"The most commonplace tavern
is dedicated to deceiving the eye."*

——THE ARCADES PROJECT

1

Your bartender story
reminded me of

```
* * * * * * * * * * *
*                   *
*      Stan's       *
*                   *
*      Tavern       *
*                   *
* * * * * * * * * * *
```

I was surprised
my father wanted
to go along
while I shot these
photographs.

"shadow

"mirror

"the blank piece of paper

"I   "went   "back

where shots (Wilson's
Union label)
and beers
reigned supreme.

2

"rummaged "Return

"disquieting "light

Your Aunt Edna,
when she first got
married, lived
just down this street.

No ice

teas or orange

blossoms here.

3

Bartending is easy in these places.

"e   "evaluation\"eyes
"t   "translate
"h   "his\"her [possessive pronoun]
"n   "native\"nationality
"o   "organize
"l   "language\"life
"o   "outside
"g   "getting\"getting\"got it all
"y   "[wh]y

My father, in his silver
Oldsmobile Achieva,
is just outside this frame.

4

December 27, 1917:
"I made it a point of honor
"to think about   *"what I am*
"here to do.

      The owner
of the bar
across the street from this one
asks, "You the guy
who took
pictures here yesterday?"

My Friend, Hank Lodowski,
had "avoiding to buy a round"
to a science.

        I try to explain
my project *"About the need*
"to collect many documents.

& he starts remembering
"the old neighborhood."

5

Since Hank never worked,
cash was always short.

"outside of   *"my work*

"seclusion

"something

"I   *"looked*   *"through*

"knowing

"reciprocated
        Dad said
his father
took him   here
to meet his work-buddies
from the railroad.

6

To be able to
drink yourself into oblivion

"intenser than
"before

over a six

or seve[n] hour period
and with p-ssing off
your buddies
                took some guts,
thought, preparation
and a system.

This is more
my old neighborhood
than theirs,

"taken down the day before

where I came
around midnight, when
I got off from work
at the restaurant.

7

We shot this photo
from the parking lot
of a car wash.

**to start, Sonny
(Hank's nickname)
came in early**
                    before
**most of the guys
arrived.**

Trains\rolled\back
behind the camera.

December 29, 1917:
"Eyes tired (field
"of vision like a screen).

8

December 27, 1917:
"I have a general idea
"about their life . . .

He bought an early
round when only
1 or 2 guys were there.

". . . and some acquaintance
"with their language . . .

Asked inside, we
talk about our project
& have our first Labatt's Blue
of the afternoon.

". . . and if I can only
"somehow 'document'
"all this, I'll have
"valuable material.

9

We're asked
what we're doing here
but not asked
inside.

"alternate

"social

"representations

**From then as new people
joined the group
they bought rounds.**

10

**Hank payed close attention
to everyone's drinks**

𝕳ere's the church

and drank accordingly.

𝕳ere's the steeple

Almost all the bars
down this street
have closed.

𝕺pen the doors

Fewer folks working
at the market, fewer
downing a couple
shots & beers at the end
of their days.

𝕾ee all the people

"The clear sky

"the promise he did not keep

11

"Return

"around

"y[our]

"story

The trick was to have
just enough to ask for another

I used to dance here
all the time, polka dances,
with your mother.

and not enough to need one
when someone
finally bought a round.

12

Sonny's famous words
for which we remember him
to this day (with fondness

for his ingenuity) was
"back me up".

The film ends here. *"vanishes*

We decide to shoot some

pool & have a few more Blues.

13

I shot photos from this angle
on several consecutive days.

December 28, 1917:
"(I felt weak, exhausted,
"my brain didn't function properly).
"Then disorganization . . .

By the time the party
broke up and we were all
broke,
       Sonny
at times with great
generosity   **offered to buy**
the remaining guys
a drink
       with the upside down
shot glasses
before him
(his back-up drinks).

14

We used to go see
Stan himself
wrestle at this place,

"paper

**Sometimes he said
goodnight and goodbuy
and stayed to polish off
his backups   himself.**

"shadow

they used to wrestle
right there
in the front window.

"wandering around

15

December 27, 1917:
"But the packing took
"a long time.
"After lunch I again
"rummaged in my things.

Before I left to catch
the train I took
this photograph.

Sonny   was a genius.

NOTE: Boldface quotations are a direct transcription of a story communicated to me (via e-mail) by Ed Michalski. Underlined dates and italicized quoted materials are taken from Bronislaw Malinowski's 1917-18 journals, published (posthumously) in *A Diary in the Strict Sense of the Term* (Routledge, 1967). The dates in the journals themselves that material is taken from, December 26-31, 1917, correspond to the exact dates (in 1997) I shot the accompanying photographs and did field-work in Buffalo, NY. A Super-8 film of this collecting experience, *Only Ask the Sick* (directed by David Michalski) is often shown as accompaniment to any reading of this text/viewing of these photos. All other material in the text is taken from my fieldnotes and from memory. Names, as standard practice dictates, are pseudonyms.

Glossary of Polish Terms

baba—old woman, grandmother

babka—grandmother (also a
   traditional Polish bread/cake)

charakter pisma—handwriting

droga—road

dworzec—(rail) station, depot

grób—grave, tomb

Grzech Pierworodny—original sin

jutro—tomorrow

krawcowa—seamstress, dressmaker

lamować—border

markotno—sullen, in low spirits

matka—mother

moje świadectwo—my testimony

na około—all around

nie nazwany—anonymous, not named

niżej—lower, below

nowiutki—brand-new

noworoczny—New Year's Day

nowo urodzny—newborn

nowy—new

nowy rok—New Year

obliczać czas—time (verb)

oczekiwać—expect, anticipate

oczekiwanie—anticipation, expectation

odwrotny—vice versa, opposite

odzew—echo, reply

oko—eye

okruch—crumb, morsel

okulary—eyeglasses

piosenka—song

potomek—descendant

powoli—slowly

pytanie—question

ranek—morning, daybreak

rozum—reason, wisdom

również—likewise, also

samotnik—solitary, recluse

skrzyżowanie—crossing

skutek—consequence

sprawdzić—verify, examine

stacja—station, stopping place

straszak—scarecrow

stworzenie—creation

teoria—theory

tutaj—here

ulewa—rainstorm

walać—soil, stain

warstwa—layer, coat

woda—water

wróżba—omen

wszyscy na raz—all at once

wzorek—pattern, model

zakończenie—ending, termination

zakorzenić się—get roots in, take roots

żałować—repent, mourn

zapalić się—ignite, set fire

zboże—corn, grain of all types

zdarzenie—incident, occurrence

ziemniak—potato

żniwo—harvest

zwiastowanie—proclamation, Annunciation

zwyczaj—custom

COLOPHON

Revenants was designed on a Macintosh with Quark XPress software at
Coffee House Press in the Warehouse District of downtown Minneapolis.
The text was set in Spectrum with four lines of Linotext on page 115.